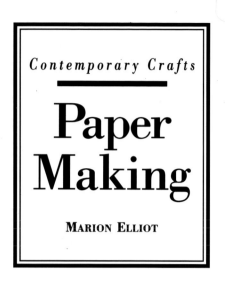

Contemporary Crafts

Paper Making

MARION ELLIOT

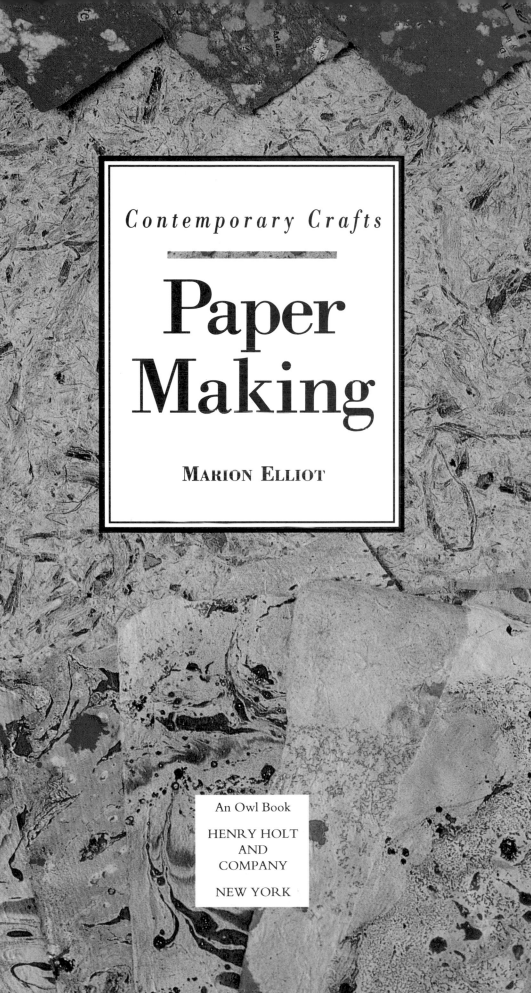

Contemporary Crafts

Paper Making

MARION ELLIOT

An Owl Book

HENRY HOLT
AND
COMPANY

NEW YORK

Henry Holt and Company, LLC
Publishers since 1866
115 West 18th Street
New York, New York 10011

Henry Holt® is a registered
trademark of Henry Holt and Company, LLC

First published in the United States in 1995 by
Henry Holt and Company, LLC
Published in Canada by Fitzhenry & Whiteside Ltd.,
195 Allstate Parkway, Markham, Ontario L3R 4T8.

Originally published in England in 1994 by
Letts of London, an imprint of New Holland (Publishers) Ltd.

Library of Congress Catalog Card Number: 94-74588

ISBN 0-8050-3895-7

Henry Holt books are available for special promotions and
premiums. For details contact: Director, Special Markets.

First American/Owl Book Edition – 1995

Designed and edited by Anness Publishing Ltd.
Editorial Director: Joanna Lorenz
Project Editor: Clare Nicholson
Design: Blackjacks
Photographer: John Freeman

Printed and bound in Singapore

5   7   9   10   8   6   4

The author and publishers have made every effort to ensure that all
the instructions contained in this book are accurate and safe, and
therefore cannot accept liability for any resulting injury, damage or
loss to persons or property however it may arise.

CONTENTS

INTRODUCTION 7

MATERIALS AND EQUIPMENT 10

BASIC TECHNIQUES 14

GALLERY 19

PROJECTS

RECYCLED PAPER 27

ONION-SKIN PAPER 33

DAFFODIL PAPER 37

LAMINATED LEAF PAPER 43

EMBOSSED WRITING PAPER 47

STENCILLED CARD 51

BIRD BOX 57

CAST BROOCHES 63

WATERMARKED LANTERN 69

PAPER-LEAF FRIEZE 73

PULP BOWL 79

TEXTURED-PAPER WALLHANGING 83

MARBLED PAPER 95

SUPPLIERS 94

ACKNOWLEDGEMENTS 95

INDEX 96

INTRODUCTION

THE CRAFT OF paper making was first developed in China, during the early part of the second century AD, by Ts'ai Lun, an official at the court of the Emperor Ho Ti. He discovered that he could break down materials – like old rags, remnants of fishing nets and plants such as mulberry and hemp – into single fibres, by pounding them in water to produce a pulpy substance. When this pulp was collected on a woven cloth stretched across a frame, and left to drain, it formed a matted material which dried as paper.

Before Ts'ai Lun's discovery of 'true' paper, that is, a material formed from the single pulped fibres of plant material and waste matter, a wide variety of writing surfaces had been used. The Egyptians, for example, wrote and drew on papyrus from around 2000 BC. This was a thin board made by layering slivers of the papyrus plant which grew in abundance along the banks of the River Nile. The layers were placed at right angles to each other and pressed, before being dried in the sun. Papyrus was also widely used by the Greeks and Romans, and was finally superseded by paper in about only the tenth century AD. In other countries, bark, the pith of certain trees, animal skins (used to make parchment and vellum), leaves, bamboo strips and cloth all served as writing surfaces.

The paper mill at Wookey Hole in Somerset, England. After pressing, large sheets of hand-made paper are hung to dry in the drying loft.

. . . .

Ts'ai Lun's invention spread throughout China, and paper was adopted for a variety of religious and secular purposes. For instance, strips of paper were substituted as 'spirit money' in place of coins in the tombs of the dead, and paper became a cheap alternative to the lengths of silk and cotton which had previously been used for scrolls.

Ts'ai Lun's basic technique was developed and improved by his apprentice, so that, by around AD 300, paper was a readily accepted writing surface. The Chinese kept their paper-making techniques a closely guarded secret for several centuries. Eventually, however, the information spread to Japan via Buddhist monks who carried books containing pages made of mulberry-leaf paper. Once introduced, the craft spread rapidly, and refinements such as the incorporation of the gampi plant into pulp were made. The Japanese also recycled previously used paper to make new sheets.

Paper making spread from the Far East in about the middle of the eighth century AD during a war between China and Persia (now Iran). Among a group of Chinese taken prisoner at Samarkand were skilled paper makers, who were forced to divulge their secret to their captors. From here, their method of making paper spread to India, Egypt and the Holy Land, finally reaching Xativa, in Spain, where a paper mill was established. So, roughly one thousand years after its discovery, paper was produced for the first time in Europe.

However, Europeans held parchment and vellum in very high esteem, and paper was not

The ancient Egyptians formed a writing material from the papyrus plant (Cyperus papyrus). *The stalks were split open and the fibrous material at the centre removed. This was cut into slithers which were laid side by side to form a long strip. A second layer was placed on top at right angles. The whole strip was then soaked in water and beaten or pressed to bond the material together.*

. . . .

an immediate success. Oriental paper was made from the fibres of local plants, and these produced a soft, absorbent material which, while ideal for the camel-hair brushes used in Chinese calligraphy, was not so suitable for the relatively sharp nibs of quill pens. In response to these difficulties, a harder paper was developed using pulped cotton rags and linen as the main ingredients. When dry, these sheets of paper were sized, or sealed, with a gelatine solution made by rendering down animal bones. This produced opaque, non-absorbent paper which was perfect for the quill pen.

During the fifteenth century, the Renaissance revolutionized thinking in the West. One of the by-products of this was a general upsurge and interest in literacy. This change was further compounded by the development of simple printing processes, initially using wooden blocks. Increased learning meant that paper gradually became an indispensable part of everyday life. The publication of the German Johannes Gutenberg's Bible in around 1450, which was printed using his own movable type, heralded the beginning of book printing in Europe. It was now possible to print illustrated books too, using woodblocks. In 1486, the first hand-tinted, illustrated English book, *The Bokys of Hauking and Huntyng* by Juliana Berners, was published. Within fifty years of Gutenberg's Bible, handbills, certificates and a host of other bureaucratic documents were being printed in large numbers.

Paper mills were in production all over Europe at this time. By 1400, such mills were working in France, Italy (most famously at Fabriano), Germany and Flanders. And in 1495, the first paper mill was established in Hertfordshire, England, by John Tate. These European mills used manufacturing processes which were very similar to those of the East, although some were rationalized to improve production. European paper contained more rags than the plant-rich papers of China and

Japan (indeed, the Great Plague is thought to have been brought to England by fleas living in the large quantities of rags imported for paper making). An Arab innovation, the use of foot-powered trip hammers to macerate the basic ingredients of the pulp, was improved upon by the Spanish paper makers of Xativa, who developed water-driven stamping mills. These consisted of rows of enormous wooden hammers, which fell rhythmically on to vats of soaked rags, pulping them quickly with a great saving of labour. This pulping method was used until the Dutch developed a revolutionary alternative in the seventeenth century. Paper-making moulds were also adapted, although the essential design remained the same. Moulds with a removable mesh made from fine bamboo or grass strips were originally used by the Japanese. A lack of suitable plant substitutes led European paper makers to use thin wire to form the mesh, which was permanently attached to the frame.

Seventeenth-century Holland was famous for the quality of its hand-made paper, and gave its name to the Hollander Beater, which was invented in 1680. This machine consisted of a large wooden tub with a revolving roller fitted with cutting blades, which pounded and ground rags against a stone plate. The beater

revolutionized the production of pulp. Rags could be broken down without requiring any pre-soaking, and the processing time from rag to pulp was very much reduced.

Speeding up pulp production made paper more economical to produce, and therefore cheaper to buy. This, in turn, led to an increase in demand which could not be maintained by the available supply of rags. It was obvious to paper manufacturers that a more readily obtainable raw material was needed, and fibres from a variety of sources were tested. These included jute, seaweed, straw, and eventually wood-pulp, which, in a refined state, is used for commercially made paper to this day.

All paper was made by hand until the beginning of the nineteenth century, with the arrival of Nicholas Louis Roberts's paper-making machine, followed by the more sophisticated Fourdrinier machine of 1806. These machines were capable of making immensely long rolls of paper, reproducing all the processes which a paper maker performed manually, and they effectively mechanized the industry.

The demand for hand-made paper has not dwindled, however; it is now more popular than ever. Artists, especially printmakers, have always prized the individuality of hand-made papers. Many prefer to use rag papers, because chemicals used in wood-based pulp can cause discoloration and eventual disintegration. The surge of interest in environmental issues has also led to a huge demand for commercially made recycled papers. These beautiful papers have inspired many to experiment with ways of making their own paper, and the simplicity of the processes involved have helped to give paper making its status of one of the most accessible and deeply satisfying crafts.

The Chinese were the first to make paper and the technique was introduced to Japan by Buddhist monks in about the seventh century AD. The Japanese experimented with the medium and developed the use of indigenous plants, such as gampi and mitsumata, to make thin, durable paper.

. . . .

MATERIALS AND EQUIPMENT

ALTHOUGH YOU can buy paper-making equipment, such as a deckle and mould, from specialist shops, you will probably find that you already possess most of the materials and equipment that you need. The basic essentials and their function are listed here; individual projects detail specific requirements.

WASTE PAPER

Some papers are much more suitable for recycling than others. Most successful are those of fairly high quality such as computer print-out paper, writing paper and brown wrapping paper. Heavily printed, highly acidic papers such as newsprint should be avoided because their high ink content will render the pulp an unattractive grey. The resulting paper will also, because of the acid, be prone to rapid discoloration and disintegration. Always remove paper clips, staples, glued edges, sticky tape and so on before using waste paper.

BLENDER

Waste paper must be macerated to break it down into pulp. It is easiest to use an electric blender but you can do it by hand with a pestle and mortar as an alternative. With a blender, mix *small* handfuls of soaked waste paper with plenty of water (the flask should be about two-thirds full of water) using 8–10-second bursts

of power. Always check that the machine is properly insulated, and rest it frequently to avoid over-heating the motor. Never operate the blender with wet hands.

MEASURING JUG

A measuring jug is useful for adding water to the blender, and also for adding water to the vat if you wish to thin the pulp at a later stage.

DECKLE AND MOULD

The most important element of the paper maker's equipment is the mould. Most paper-making moulds come in two separate pieces. The first, a mesh-covered wooden frame, is called the mould. This is complemented by an open wooden frame of exactly the same proportions, which is known as a deckle. The deckle fits over the mould, which is held mesh-side up. Pulp is scooped on to the frame from a vat, and excess water drains through the mesh to leave a deposit which dries as paper. The deckle shapes the sides of the paper sheet by trapping the pulp. The characteristic look of hand-made paper, with its wavy 'deckle' edge, is caused by small amounts of pulp seeping through the slight gap between mould and deckle.

There are two types of mould covering. 'Laid' moulds have a screen made from closely spaced brass wires. These give 'laid' paper its slightly ridged surface. 'Wove' moulds are covered with a woven mesh surface. This produces slightly smoother paper. Although professional paper makers generally favour moulds covered with woven brass screens, these tend to be prohibitively expensive. Net curtaining, silk-screen fabric, or any fairly fine-woven nylon mesh will work well.

Deckles and moulds may be home-made or shop-bought and they can be constructed quite easily from wood. The inside dimensions of the frame will determine the size of the paper. To make the mould take four lengths of wood cut to size and join them at the corners with water-proof glue and brass screws. The corners can be strengthened with brass L-shaped corner plates. The mould is then covered with mesh which must be stretched as taut as possible in both directions. Secure the mesh with nails or staples. The deckle should be made to exactly the same size as the mould and assembled in the same way but without the mesh. Apply two coats of waterproof varnish to the deckle and mould before use.

VAT

The vat, which is used to hold pulp suspended in water, should be large enough to accommodate a deckle and mould comfortably. A rectangular photographic tray makes a good vat, as does a large washing-up bowl. Prepared pulp should be added to a vat of clean water roughly in the ratio of one part pulp to four parts water. The higher the proportion of pulp to water, the thicker the sheet of paper will be. More pulp should be added to the vat at regular intervals during paper making to replenish the supply, and the contents mixed frequently with a wooden spoon.

If you have any pulp left over at the end of a session, you can drain it through a sieve and store it in an airtight container for up to two weeks. Never dispose of pulp down the sink, because it is very likely to block the drain. Instead, sieve it to remove excess water and then throw it away.

WOODEN SPOON

When more pulp is added to the vat the contents should be mixed thoroughly with a wooden spoon. This will ensure even distribution of fibres, as the pulp will quickly fall to the bottom of the vat.

COUCHING FELTS AND KITCHEN CLOTHS

After each new sheet of paper is formed on the mould, it is transferred to a piece of damp fabric, traditionally pure wool, known as a felt. This process is called couching. Felts act as a support for wet paper, and also absorb some of the moisture. They must be damp so that the paper can be transferred smoothly from mould to fabric – if the felt is not wet enough, parts of the new sheet may get left behind on the mould mesh. Each sheet of paper is interleaved with a felt, and the pile of felts and paper is called a post. The first sheet of paper may be couched on to a flat felt, or on to a slightly curved pad of felts known as the couching mound. Good alternatives to pure-wool felts are pieces of blanket, fine towelling, or kitchen cloths.

PRESSING BOARDS AND G-CLAMPS

Once a post of hand-made paper has been formed, the sheets are pressed to expel as much water as possible and to bond the fibres together. During the pressing, the paper needs to be protected between two boards. The boards should be slightly larger than the sheets of paper, and should be held tightly together with g-clamps or long screws with wing nuts. Before they are used for the first time, the pressing boards should be sealed with two coats of polyurethane or acrylic varnish.

BUCKET

If a large quantity of waste paper is to be recycled, it should be soaked overnight in water until it starts to disintegrate. This will make the pulping process much easier. If the paper is very heavyweight, you may need to add hot water to accelerate the process. If this is the case, the bucket should not be made of plastic.

NEWSPAPER

Newspaper is very useful for absorbing water during paper pressing and for supporting felts and drying paper. It may also be used in place of felts to make a couching mound.

DRYING SURFACE

Any non-absorbent material such as Perspex (Plexiglas) or Formica makes a good drying surface for damp paper once it has been pressed, and allows the paper to dry without warping, wrinkling or buckling.

SIEVE

A sieve is useful for draining pulp and plant matter before further processing.

PLASTIC TRAY

When marbling paper you need a shallow plastic tray just larger than the size of the paper you are marbling. It is also useful to have some sort of plastic container to hand when paper making involves working with pulp, rather than pulling a sheet of paper.

RUBBER GLOVES

Rubber or disposable plastic gloves protect the hands from staining – printed or coloured waste paper tends to release a lot of ink once it has been soaked, which can be difficult to remove from the skin.

Heavy plastic protective gloves should always be used when handling boiled plant matter to prevent scalding. They should also be worn if chemicals are being used to break down plant fibres.

GOGGLES

Always wear protective goggles if you are breaking down plant fibres with chemicals.

PVA (WHITE) GLUE

Glue may be added in small quantities to the vat of pulp before the first sheet of paper is pulled. This will act as a size, sealing the surface of the paper and rendering it suitable for writing on.

BLENDER

KITCHEN CLOTHS

MEASURING JUG

COUCHING FELTS

PLASTIC TRAY

BUCKET

VAT

G-CLAMPS

WOODEN SPOON

MOULD

PRESSING BOARDS

DECKLE

NEWSPAPER

PVA (WHITE) GLUE

SIEVE

GOGGLES

PLASTIC GLOVES

BASIC TECHNIQUES

BEFORE YOU PULL a sheet of paper, you need to put prepared pulp into the vat. Remember that the ratio should be roughly one part pulp to four parts water. Once you have agitated the pulp thoroughly with a wooden spoon, you can start the real paper-making process.

PULLING A SHEET OF PAPER

First, dampen the mesh of the paper-making mould with water so that the pulp will drain easily. Hold the screen vertically, so that it faces you, with the mesh facing upwards and the deckle held firmly in place on top of the mould. Lower the screen into the near side of the vat and gently push it away from you. As you do so, gradually submerge the frame until it lies flat under the surface of the water. Keeping the mould horizontal and steady, remove it from the vat and, before all the water drains away, shake it gently backwards and forwards. This will mesh the fibres together, ensuring strong paper.

Rest the mould and deckle on one corner of the vat for about 20 seconds to drain the pulp. Then tilt it slightly for another few seconds to remove as much water as possible. Now remove the deckle and put it to one side. Make sure that you do not drip water on to the wet paper as this will spoil the surface.

If you prefer, you can also make paper by collecting pulp on the mould without the deckle, but this will result in sheets with more

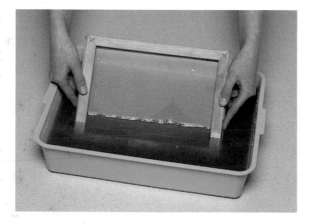

Start pulling a sheet of paper by lowering the mould (with the mesh face-up and the deckle on top) into the side of the vat nearest to you. Then gently submerge the frame while pulling it towards you.

. . . .

Once the mould has been submerged in the pulp-and-water mixture, lift it out with both hands, keeping it horizontal. Before the water drains, shake the mould backwards and forwards. Do not be too vigorous.

. . . .

When you have drained the mould and deckle for about 20 seconds, carefully remove the deckle. Take care not to let any drips of water fall from it on to the paper or they will spoil the finished result.

. . . .

uneven edges. If for any reason you feel that the paper is unsatisfactory, return the pulp to the vat, mix it well and start again.

COUCHING PAPER

Couching a sheet of paper means transferring it from the mould on which it has formed on to a damp, thick piece of fabric which will support the paper as it dries. You may couch paper flat on to the fabric, or on to a slightly curved pad known as a 'couching mound'. The mound can be made from folded felts or a combination of newspaper and felts. A couching mound gives more support to the first few sheets of paper, and should be removed before the paper is pressed flat. Couching fabric is traditionally 100 per cent wool felt, but blanket, towelling, or woven-paper kitchen cloths are good alternatives. The felts should be wet but not saturated.

To couch a piece of paper, hold the mould almost vertically to the right of the felt with the pulp facing down. Then transfer the paper on to the felt in one smooth rolling action. Press the mould quite hard on to the felt so that the pulp adheres. Continue the rolling action to lift the empty mould from the felt once the paper has been couched. Cover the first sheet of paper with another wet felt. When you have pulled a second sheet, couch it on top of this. Continue to interleave paper and felts until the 'post' (the technical term for a pile of felts and paper) is finished. Cover the final sheet of paper with a felt.

To couch a sheet of paper so that it can dry, transfer it from the mesh of the mould on to a suitable damp cloth. Press quite firmly and use a smooth, rolling action to push down and then lift up the mould.

. . . .

RECYCLING PAPER

Many types of paper may be recycled satisfactorily, provided that they are not too heavily glazed and glossy, waxy, or acidic. The more processed and opaque the paper, the less water it will absorb, and the longer it will take to disintegrate. Highly acidic paper such as newsprint has a very high wood-pulp content and makes recycled paper which discolours badly, and eventually falls apart.

Waste paper should be torn into postage-stamp-sized squares and covered with water. Soaking quickly breaks down the paper, which becomes mushy. Soaking times vary and may be speeded up by adding hot water to the pulp bucket. Better-quality, thicker papers, such as watercolour paper, may require two or more days' soaking, whereas tissue will break down rapidly. Generally speaking, an overnight soak will be long enough for most papers.

Thoroughly rinse the soaked paper in clean water before you blend it. If only a small quantity of pulp is required – enough for just one sheet of paper, for example – you can blend unsoaked paper successfully with plenty of clean water.

BLENDING PULP

If you plan to use an electric blender to macerate recycled paper, you *must* follow certain safety procedures. As pulping involves the use of water, it is essential that the blender is properly insulated, and you should take care not to let pools develop on the work surface. Never use the machine with wet hands, or switch it on and leave it to blend unattended. Also, once used for pulping, do not use the blender flask for food preparation. Place *small* handfuls of soaked paper in the flask of the blender, which should be about two-thirds full of clean water. Blend the paper using short bursts of power, of no more than 8–10 seconds, as it is important not to over-heat the motor. It is wise to let the machine rest frequently between blendings to avoid any strain. Do not blend pulp to too smooth a consistency, or the resulting paper will lack strength. If you prefer, you can break down soaked paper manually in a pestle and mortar.

ADDITIONS TO PULP

You can add a variety of ingedients to pulp to produce paper with an interesting surface texture. Especially good for this are organic materials such as seeds, leaves, flower petals, dried herbs, tea leaves and silk threads. You can also colour pulp by adding non-toxic powder paint to the vat.

PRESSING A POST OF PAPER

After a post of paper has been formed, it should be placed between two boards and pressed. This process helps to bond the wet fibres together before the sheets are removed from their cloths and dried. There are several methods of pressing paper; for instance, you can simply sandwich the post between two waterproofed boards and stand on top for 10 minutes or so. Then you need to lay heavy objects such as house bricks on top, gradually increasing the pressure until most of the water has been expelled. A book binder's press is perfect for applying this gradual pressure; alternatively, you can attach g-clamps to the boards and slowly tighten them. Whichever method you use, most of the excess water should be expelled from the wet paper and felts in about 30 minutes, after which you should take the post out from between the pressing boards. Copious amounts of water will be expelled from the wet paper and felts during pressing, so, if possible, you should do this outside. Otherwise, have plenty of cloths to soak up the water, and work near a sink.

DRYING THE PAPER

After you have removed the post from between the boards, separate it into single felts, each supporting a sheet of damp paper. To dry the felts, you can simply leave them on sheets of newspaper at room temperature, but you will need to replace the newspaper frequently as it absorbs the excess water. Alternatively, transfer the sheets to a non-absorbent surface, such as Perspex (Plexiglas) or Formica; this will speed the drying time. Do not place the damp sheets near an artificial heat source, as this may cause unsightly warping due to uneven drying. Once the paper is dry, which may take anything up to a week depending on the room temperature and weather conditions, carefully peel the sheets from their drying surface and stack them between boards until they are needed. If the paper is unsized at this stage it is known as waterleaf, and is highly absorbent.

SIZING THE PAPER

You can add size to paper either externally or internally during the making process. For the internal method, add household starch, PVA (white) glue or commercially prepared size to the pulp while it is in the vat. One or two tablespoons of starch or glue per vat of pulp should be sufficient. Follow the manufacturer's instructions if you are using commercial size.

External sizing is carried out on dried paper after it has been allowed to 'cure' for several weeks. This maturing period strengthens the paper, so that it is less likely to disintegrate during sizing. Dissolve about one teaspoon of gelatine or a non-animal alternative, such as agar-agar, in 1 litre (1¾ pints / 2 US pints) of hot water and pour it into a shallow tray. Dip each sheet quickly in the sizing tray and lay it on a felt. It is important that the dipping is done before the gelatine cools and hardens, and therefore only small amounts of size should be mixed at a time. When all the sheets of paper are sized, put them to a non-absorbent surface to dry. Then wash the felts in warm soapy water to remove all traces of size.

PREPARING PLANT FIBRES

A variety of plants may be used to make paper. Long-fibred plants which prove successful include asparagus, daffodils, rhubarb, celery and spinach. Plants vary according to their age, the soil type in which they have been grown and so on, and no two will take the same length of time to break down. Fresh or dried plant matter may be used; once flowers have finished, you can hang them upside-down until you are ready to use them. Some plants will disintegrate with gentle boiling in plenty of clean water. Others have tougher fibres which require chemicals, such as soda ash (sodium carbonate), to break them down. You may have to order these chemicals from a chemist (drug store). The ratio of soda ash to plant fibre is 20 per cent ash to the dry weight of the plant material. A 200 g (7 oz) sample of plant material will need 40 g / 1½ oz ash, diluted in 3 litres (5¼ pints / 6⅓ US pints) water. Work in a well-ventilated room, on a stove which is not used for domestic purposes, and wear protective clothing. Boil the plant material in a stainless-steel saucepan for four to five hours, stirring every half hour. Leave to cool, then rinse thoroughly until the water runs off clear.

As with paper pulp, softened plant fibres need to be macerated to reduce them to single fibres, and to release the cellulose stored inside which helps to bond the paper together. The best way to process boiled plants is to beat them with a wooden rolling pin or mallet on a wooden chopping block. The more the pulp is beaten, the finer the paper will be – about 20 minutes' beating is usually adequate.

GALLERY

The makers whose work appears in this gallery all have one thing in common – they use paper – but the applications of this basic material are astonishing in their variety. The paper has been collaged, moulded, torn, cut, stitched, cast, stretched, painted and dyed, and takes on completely new and unexpected qualities. Nearly all the artists recycle their paper from waste materials, creating a wonderfully rich variety of textures, colours and surface patterns which underline the fundamental beauty and versatility of the material. All these elements will prove an exciting starting point for the novice paper maker. Experimentation and exploration are the key words in the art of paper making. Try a variety of techniques and ideas to create both functional and decorative paper items.

~

Fishes – Paper Collage
SHIRLEY BRINSLEY
Shirley draws inspiration for her work from a wide variety of sources, and finds folk art especially interesting. Her paper collages often reflect her concern with environmental themes and disappearing cultures. Shirley dyes, tears and cuts her own hand-made paper – and waste papers such as interesting packaging – to make brightly coloured, highly illustrative collages. She sometimes over-stitches the paper to add colourful details and the various surface textures which give her work its rich, densely patterned appearance.

Wallhanging

ELIZABETH COUZINS

Elizabeth uses all sorts of simple plastic objects as moulds, casting thin paper shapes from them. She colours the casts, adding found items such as copper washers, pieces of wire and scraps of brightly coloured tissue paper and silk to make richly textured, opulent pieces of paper. She then incorporates these into wallhangings, friezes, and sometimes jewellery.

. . . .

Jewellery

SHIRLEY BRINSLEY

Shirley's richly decorative jewellery is made by layering small pieces of hand-made paper on to cardboard shapes which are then varnished several times to give a smooth lacquered surface. Occasionally she adds metal leaf to give a flash of vibrant detail.

. . . .

Voladores II

JEAN DAVEY-WINTER

This piece is made from
individually pulled sheets
of paper. Jean adds yarn
to the basic pulp for
extra decorative texture.
Some areas of the work
are printed, embossed
and waxed. The surface
has a weathered,
distressed appearance,
and is embellished with
fragments of photo-
graphs taken in the Vera
Cruz region of Mexico.
The photographs show
an ancient fertility rite
performed by a troupe
of voladores.
. . . .

Bowl

JACQUELINE OLDFIELD

Jacqueline formed this
delicate, luminous bowl
by layering dyed paper
pulp into a mould. Its
surface is inlaid with
various fibres and then
decorated with acrylic
paints. The bowl is
varnished to strengthen
the paper, and to make
it watertight.
. . . .

Paper Piece

JACQUELINE OLDFIELD

Much of Jacqueline's work is inspired by the surface textures and natural decay found in architecture. The papers in this piece are made by gathering hand-dyed pulp directly on to a piece of shaped wire mesh to make an unusual 'organic' surface reminiscent of stone. The papers are joined, and embroidery threads are stitched over the surface for extra interest.

. . . .

Turtle

GERRY COPP

This vibrant, wonderfully strange turtle is made on a wood-and-cardboard armature which has been packed out with papier mâché. Each part of its body is inspired by a different sea-creature. The legs are based on anemones, the body on a fish, and only the head on a turtle. The basic papier-mâché shape has been embellished with cut and torn handmade papers and decorative detail has been added with coloured pens.

. . . .

Recycled Paper

VANESSA GODFREY

Vanessa recycles waste paper into a pulp which she then divides into small batches and colours with bright pigments. Working directly on the screen mesh, she masks areas with newspaper, and 'draws' with the pulp to create a vivid, lively design. She may also trail water over portions of the pulp to make textured areas. The paper is left to air-dry on the frame, a process which may take a few days or weeks, depending on the weather.

. . . .

Hand-made Paper

MARA AMATS

Mara is a highly skilled paper maker; she has set up several paper-making projects in developing countries to help local people generate income from the plants growing abundantly around them. Sales of this paper in the USA and UK have paid for such essentials as schools, medical clinics and pension plans for the paper makers. This 'sample sheet' is made from water hyacinths overlaid with leaves from the sacred bodhi tree, and a cast taken from a fan.

. . . .

Pleated Paper

MARA AMATS

Very fine paper has been couched and then pleated by hand to make a delicate surface which resembles fabric. The papers are dyed by hand with subtle colours which impart a rich but subdued patina.

. . . .

Stilettos

SUSAN C. CUTTS

Susan uses her own hand-made paper, which is dyed at the pulping stage, to make her three-dimensional pieces. The paper is layered and moulded while it is still wet which enables her to form her work without using any stitching or glue.

. . . .

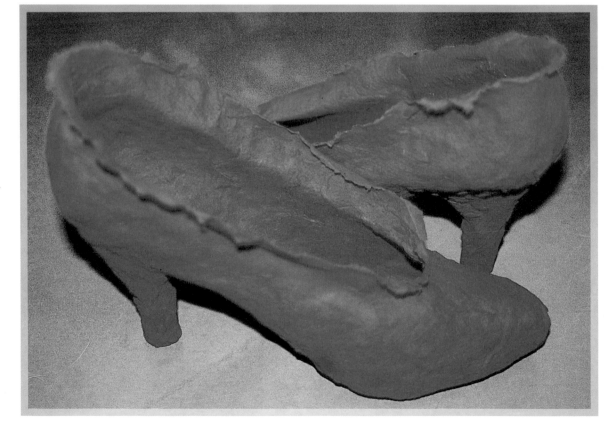

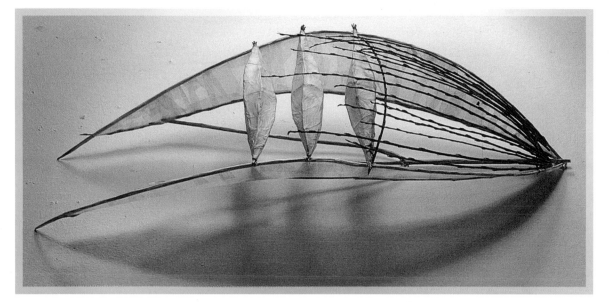

Sculptural Forms
VANESSA GODFREY
Vanessa took inspiration for these sculptural forms from organic sources such as seed pods. They are made by stretching sheets of recycled packaging tissue over a delicate frame work of wire and bamboo. Their rich colour is achieved by hand-dying the individual papers before they are applied over the frames.
. . . .

Crown, Wristcuffs, Necklaces, Earrings
GILL CLEMENT
Gill finds inspiration in the colours and decorative traditions of India and frequently visits the country to study techniques and processes. These pieces are formed entirely from hand-made Indian paper, their rich colour coming from applications of paint and gold wax. Their design reflects another of Gills's preoccupations – the rich Celtic heritage of Wales.

. . . .

RECYCLED PAPER

GERRY COPP

THE SIMPLEST WAY to make new paper is to recycle old, and the brighter the waste paper, the more exciting the resulting sheets will be. Some papers are more suitable for recycling than others, and you will discover this by experimenting with and testing different raw materials. Don't over-blend the paper, as this will produce a bland-looking pulp. Roughly processed waste paper gives more interesting, much livelier results, especially if you use highly contrasting colours.

~

MATERIALS AND EQUIPMENT

• waste paper in a variety of colours • electric blender • pulp vat • wooden spoon • deckle and mould • kitchen cloths • pressing boards • newspapers • g-clamps · · · · · ·

1 Tear the waste paper into postage-stamp-sized pieces. Blend small handfuls with plenty of water to make a pulp, resting the blender frequently to avoid over-heating the motor. It is a good idea to blend some batches of the paper more than others in order to give the pulp an interesting consistency.

2 Fill the vat with clean water. There should be about four parts of water to one part of pulp. Pour the pulp into the vat.

3 Stir the contents of the vat with the wooden spoon to distribute the pulp evenly before pulling the first sheet of paper. Hold the mould and deckle firmly together, with the mould mesh-side up. Lower the frame into the vat as shown and gradually submerge it until it is covered with a layer of pulp.

4 Keeping it horizontal, lift the frame from the vat shaking it lightly backwards and forwards to mesh the pulp together.

5 Let the frame drain for a few seconds and then rest it on one corner of the vat for a further 20 seconds. Remove the deckle and put it to one side. Be careful not to drip water on to the wet paper at this stage, as this will spoil the surface. Drain the mould for a few more seconds on the side of the vat.

6 Couch the sheet of paper on to a thin pile of damp kitchen cloths. Transfer the paper in one smooth movement, either rolling the mould towards you or away from you. Hold the mould upright at one edge of the cloth, roll it down and up the other side, leaving the paper on the cloths.

7 Cover the couched paper with another damp cloth to create a surface on to which you can couch a second sheet of paper.

8 Pull a second sheet of paper and couch it on top of the first. Again, cover the paper with a damp cloth. Continue this process until you have made a post (the stack of paper inter-leaved with damp cloths). If there is any unused pulp left over, do not dispose of it down the sink because it will block the drains. If you strain it through a sieve, you can store the pulp in an airtight container for up to two weeks.

9 Put some newspaper on one of the pressing boards, then place the post of paper on top. Cover with more newspaper and the second pressing board and clamp them together to remove as much excess water as possible. Tighten the g-clamps gradually to increase pressure on the paper. Make sure that the boards are on a thick pile of newspapers, preferably near a sink or drain, as copious amounts of water will be expressed.

10 Leave the post to press for about 30 minutes, then undo the clamps and remove the boards. Separate the post into single cloths, each supporting a sheet of paper. Lay the cloths on newspaper to dry. When the recycled paper has dried, carefully peel each sheet from its cloth.

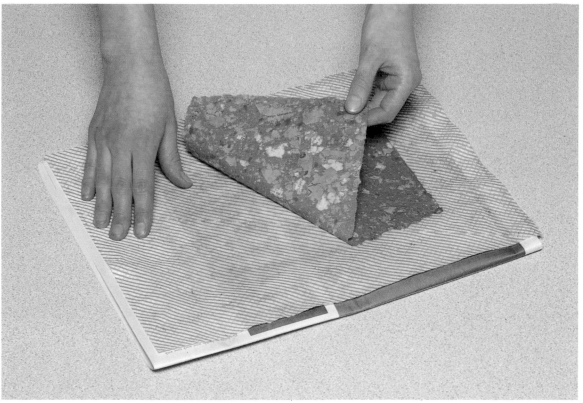

ONION-SKIN PAPER

JACQUELINE OLDFIELD

VEGETABLE SKINS and peel added to recycled-paper pulp produce an interestingly speckled surface. Onion skins are particularly effective, having a pearly translucency which is both elegant and subtle. The skins should be boiled first to prepare them and the colour they release into the water may be added to the pulp to enhance the paper with a warm hue.

~

MATERIALS AND EQUIPMENT

- *white waste paper*
- *electric blender • onions*
- *scissors • saucepan*
- *wooden spoon • pulp vat • deckle and mould*
- *kitchen cloths • pressing boards • newspapers*
- *g-clamps*

......

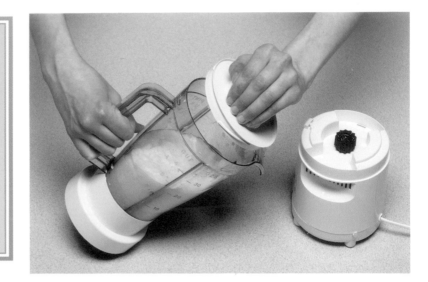

1 Tear the waste paper into postage-stamp-sized pieces and blend them with plenty of water to form a pulp. Allow the blender to rest frequently in order to avoid over-heating the motor.

2 Peel several onions and keep them for cooking purposes. Cut the onion skins into small pieces, and place them in a saucepan half-filled with water. Replenish the water if necessary during simmering.

3 Gently simmer the skins for 45 minutes, stirring occasionally, until they have released their colour into the water.

4 Add the softened skins, a few at a time, and some of the onion water, to the pulp. Blend lightly to reduce the skins in size. Take care not to over-heat the blender's motor.

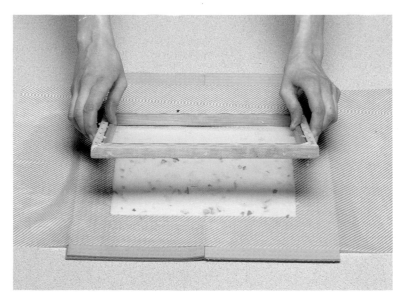

5 Tip the pulp into the vat and dilute it slightly with more water. Mix with a wooden spoon to distribute the contents evenly. Pull a sheet of paper.

6 Couch the onion paper on to a pile of damp kitchen cloths. Press the paper between two boards and newspapers sealed with g-clamps for 30 minutes to remove excess water, then leave it to dry on another cloth.

DAFFODIL PAPER

MARA AMATS

PLANTS CAN BE USED to make wonderful paper, full of interesting textures and irregularities which are a welcome antidote to the blandness of machine-made varieties. Most long-fibred plants will yield paper of immense strength and durability; experiment with a selection such as spinach, celery, asparagus, rhubarb and daffodils. Perseverence and practice will reveal which plants are most suitable. The fibres will need further beating once they have been separated by boiling. It is best to do this by hand on a wooden board, as an electric blender will cut the fibres too short, resulting in weaker paper.

~

MATERIALS AND EQUIPMENT

• *bunch of fresh or dried daffodils* • *scissors* • *saucepan* • *rubber gloves* • *sieve* • *wooden chopping block* • *wooden rolling pin* • *glass of cold water* • *pulp vat* • *wooden spoon* • *deckle and mould* • *flat, non-absorbent surface* • *palette knife (spatula)*
. . . . . .

1 Cut the daffodil stems with scissors into equal lengths of about 7.5 cm (3 in).

2 Put the stems and flowers in a saucepan and cover them completely with water. Place the pan on a stove and bring the water to the boil. Then turn down the heat and simmer the daffodils gently for 30 minutes.

3 Wearing rubber gloves, take a few daffodil stems and pull them apart. They will tear easily if they are ready; otherwise simmer them for slightly longer.

4 Drain the fibres through a sieve, then rinse them thoroughly under cold water, turning them constantly. Allow the fibres to drain again.

5 Place the rinsed fibres on a wooden chopping block, and beat them with a rolling pin to break them down. Turn and fold the plants as you work to ensure that the whole mass is processed. Continue beating until the fibres are an amorphous pulp. The more you beat the fibres, the finer the paper will be.

6 To check whether the fibres are ready, drop a sample into a glass of cold water. The fibres should blend with the water. If any large pieces sink to the bottom, the fibres need more beating. They are ready when they feel like wet strands of hair.

7 Pour the fibres into a water-filled vat. If you want to add any extra materials to the pulp, this is the stage at which they should go in. You could strengthen the paper by adding some paper pulp or you could add more flowerheads to enhance the decoration of the paper. Agitate the vat with a wooden spoon to distribute the contents and then pull a sheet of paper.

8 Couch the fibre paper on to a flat, non-absorbent surface, such as a work top, to dry. On no account dispose of any excess pulp down the sink, as it will block the drains. When the paper is dry, gently prise it from the drying surface with a palette knife (spatula). The picture shows papers made from plant fibre and dried flowerheads, plant fibre and pulp and pure plant fibre.

LAMINATED
LEAF PAPER

VANESSA GODFREY

LAMINATION DESCRIBES the process in which two sheets of paper are couched on top of each other, often with one or more objects sandwiched between the layers. All sorts of interesting items may be preserved between papers: leaf skeletons, small scraps of fabric, wrappers, stamps, flower petals or seeds all give pleasing results. In this project, leaves have been placed in a simple, unfussy pattern to emphasize their natural beauty.

~

MATERIALS AND EQUIPMENT

- *waste paper* • *electric blender* • *pulp vat*
- *wooden spoon* • *deckle and mould* • *kitchen cloths* • *newspapers*
- *variety of small leaves*
- *plastic measuring jug*
- *pressing boards*
- *g-clamps*

. . . . . .

1 Blend the waste paper with plenty of water to a pulp, processing small handfuls at a time so as not to over-heat the blender's motor. Pour the pulp into the vat and add about four parts of clean water. Stir up the mixture, then pull a sheet of paper.

2 Couch the paper on to a damp kitchen cloth placed on several sheets of newspaper.

3 Carefully arrange the leaves on the couched paper in a simple design.

4 Add water to the vat to dilute the pulp. Pull a thin sheet of paper using only the mould without the deckle. You may need several attempts to make sure that the sheet of paper is quite thin.

5 Carefully couch the second sheet of paper on to the first, sealing in the leaves, which should remain visible through the thin pulp.

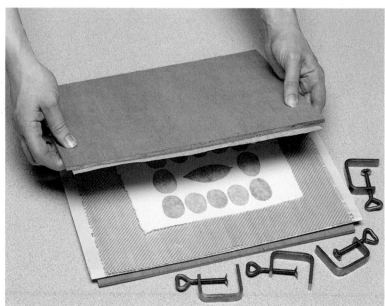

6 Transfer the couched paper and newspaper to a pressing board. Cover with a damp cloth, more newspaper and a second board. Seal with g-clamps. Replace the damp newspaper every so often, and continue pressing until the paper is dry.

Embossed Writing Paper

VANESSA GODFREY

THIS DELICATE PAPER has a raised lacy border along two sides, which is formed by 'embossing' the wet sheet. This is done by couching the paper on to strips of lace and then pressing it firmly between boards. The wet pulp retains the pattern as a low-relief border. All sorts of objects may be used to emboss paper, including simple shapes cut from cardboard.

~

MATERIALS AND EQUIPMENT

• *white waste paper*
• *electric blender* • *pulp vat* • *dessertspoon* • *PVA (white) glue* • *pressing boards* • *newspapers*
• *kitchen cloths* • *lace trimming* • *scissors*
• *wooden spoon*
• *g-clamps*
· · · · · ·

1 Blend the waste paper to a pulp with plenty of water, processing small handfuls at a time so as not to over-heat the blender's motor. Pour the pulp into the vat and add about four parts of clean water. Mix a dessertspoonful of PVA (white) glue with a little water and stir into the pulp. This will seal the surface of the paper.

2 Place a pressing board on the work surface. Lay a few sheets of folded newspaper on top, and cover with a damp kitchen cloth.

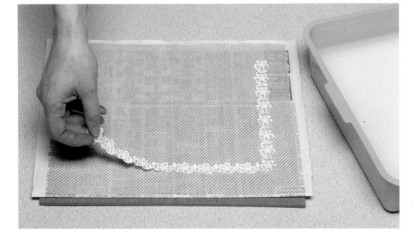

3 Cut the lace trimming to size, and lay it on the kitchen cloth.

4 Pull a sheet of paper and carefully couch it on to the kitchen cloth, covering the lace.

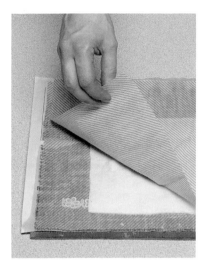

5 Cover the paper with a damp
kitchen cloth, then another
layer of newspaper. Place the
second pressing board on top.

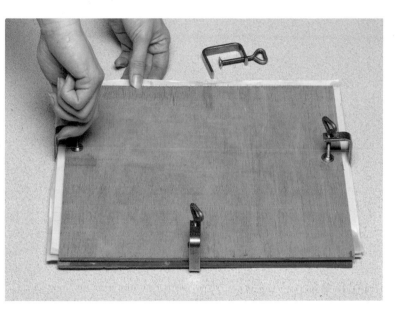

6 Fix the boards together with
g-clamps placed at regular
intervals, and tighten the clamps
gradually. Replace the newspapers
when they become damp, and
press again for about 30 minutes.

7 Remove the paper from the
boards, and lay it to dry on
a cloth. When the paper has
dried, carefully lift away the
lace trimming.

STENCILLED CARD

VANESSA GODFREY

PERSONALIZED GREETINGS CARDS may be made by stencilling simple motifs in contrasting pulps on to couched paper. The stencils are cut from sheets of fine wire mesh, and may be used many times. After each stencilling session, carefully dry and wrap the stencils in newspaper to prevent them from rusting.

~

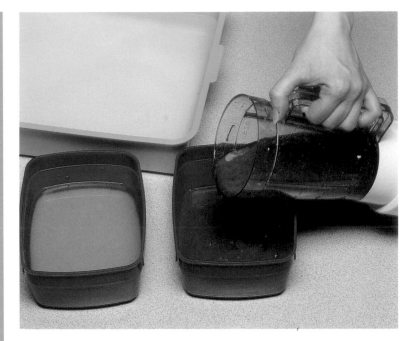

MATERIALS AND EQUIPMENT

• *waste paper in a variety of colours, including white* • *electric blender* • *pulp vat* • *small plastic tubs (one for each colour of pulp)* • *dessertspoon* • *PVA (white) glue* • *drawing paper* • *pen or pencil* • *ruler* • *scissors* • *sheet of fine wire mesh* • *newspapers* • *kitchen cloths* • *wooden spoon* • *deckle and mould* • *sponge* • *pressing boards* • *g-clamps* • *sheet of Perspex (Plexiglas), or other non-absorbent surface* • *paintbrush* • *palette knife (spatula)* • *thin card (cardboard)* • *double-sided tape*
......

1 Tear pieces of white waste paper into postage-stamp-sized pieces. Blend small handfuls with plenty of water to make a pulp. Pour this into the vat with about four parts of clean water. Next, blend smaller quantities of each different colour of waste paper, one at°a time. Pour the resulting pulp into individual plastic tubs. Mix a dessertspoonful of PVA (white) glue with a little water and stir into the white pulp in the main vat.

2 Draw a selection of simple motifs on a sheet of paper, using a ruler if you want straight lines. Cut out the shapes to make templates.

3 Hold each template in turn on the sheet of wire mesh, and carefully cut around them to make stencils.

4 Place a folded sheet of newspaper on a work top and cover it with a damp kitchen cloth. Pull a sheet of white paper and couch it on to the cloth. Dip the first stencil into one of the coloured pulps, ensuring that it is evenly covere . Allow any excess water to drain from the mesh.

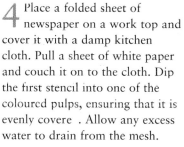

5 Carefully place the first stencil pulp-side down on to the sheet of white paper. If any fibres are caught over the edge of the mesh, gently ease them back with your finger. Use a sponge to soak up excess water, if necessary.

6 Carefully remove the stencil and repeat the process to couch the second shape – in this instance, another star.

7 Using a different stencil and coloured pulp, couch a third image to complete the design.

8 Cover the paper with a damp kitchen cloth, and press between pressing boards, fixed with g-clamps, for about 30 minutes to remove excess water. Use plenty of newspapers under the boards to absorb the water, and work by a sink if possible. Remove the paper from between the boards, still on its cloth, and place it carefully, with the stencilled side down, on a sheet of Perspex (Plexiglas) or other non-absorbent surface.

9 Use a paintbrush to smooth the back of the kitchen cloth. This will expel any air bubbles between the damp paper and the surface. Peel back the kitchen cloth, leaving the damp sheet of paper attached to the Perspex (Plexiglas). Allow the paper to dry.

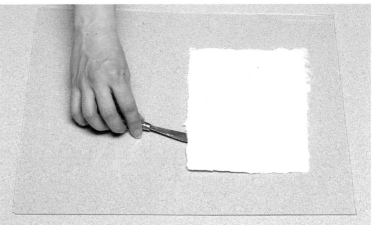

10 Slide a palette knife (spatula) gently between the surface and dry paper.

11 Fold a sheet of thin card (cardboard) in half to make the base of the greetings card, and trim the stencilled paper to size. Stick the paper design on the front half of the card with strips of double-sided tape.

BIRD BOX

GERRY COPP

THIS BRIGHTLY coloured box is decorated with recycled papers made from left-over handbills. The papers are carefully torn into strips, spots and swirls and applied all over the surface of the box and lid in a lively, cheerful design. Before the paper is sealed with clear varnish, the bird is embellished further with a delicate pattern of spots and stripes.

~

MATERIALS AND EQUIPMENT

• *waste paper in a variety of colours* • *electric blender* • *pulp vat* • *wooden spoon* • *deckle and mould* • *kitchen cloths* • *pressing boards* • *g-clamps* • *round cardboard box with lid* • *PVA (white) glue* • *glue brush* • *coloured pens* • *polyurethane or acrylic varnish* • *paintbrush* ......

1 Tear the waste paper into postage-stamp-sized pieces. Blend small handfuls of each different colour separately with plenty of water to make a pulp.

Let the blender rest frequently so that the motor does not over-heat. Pour the first batch of coloured pulp into the vat with about four parts of clean water.

2 Pull the first sheet of paper and couch it on to a pile of damp kitchen cloths. Cover with another damp cloth.

3 Pull a second sheet of paper and couch it on top of the first. Continue until you have made a number of sheets of one colour, then repeat with the other colours.

4 Press the papers between pressing boards fixed with g-clamps for about 30 minutes. Do not press sheets of different colours together as the colours might bleed into each other. When there is no more excess water, separate the post and lay out each sheet on its own cloth to dry. When the papers are thoroughly dry, peel them gently away from their cloths.

5 Carefully tear strips of contrasting paper into thick bands. Stick them to the outside of the box with PVA (white) glue. Then cover the inside of the box with paper, too.

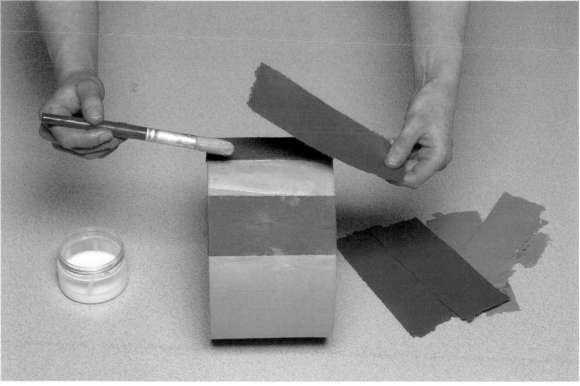

6 Tear swirls of bright paper and paste them on to the striped sides of the box in a random pattern.

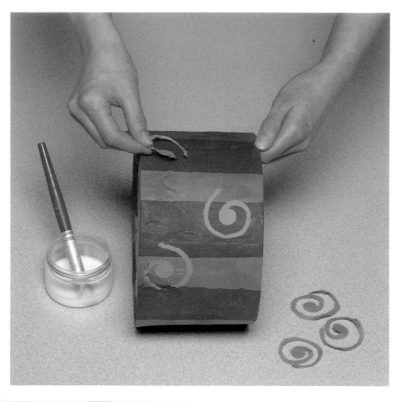

7 Decorate the lid in the same way as the main part of the box, adding bright spots of colour to the swirls. Cover the inside of the lid, too.

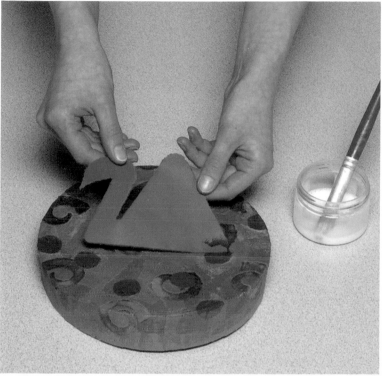

8 Carefully tear a bird shape from blue paper and paste it on to the lid. Tear smaller, contrasting pieces of paper to add decorative detail to the bird's body.

9 When the glue has dried, fill in the bird with patterns using coloured pens.

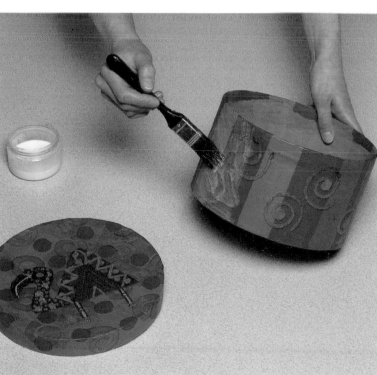

10 When the box is thoroughly dry, seal both the lid and body with a coat of polyurethane or acrylic varnish.

CAST BROOCHES

ELIZABETH COUZINS

THESE VIBRANT PIECES of jewellery are cast from humble household objects using paper pulp. They are decorated with paints, inks and crayons, and then embellished with copper wires to give an opulent, richly textured surface resembling appliqué work. All sorts of items make good moulds: both natural forms such as shells, and manufactured items such as buttons, cogs and washers can be combined or used on their own to exciting effect. Each piece is finished with a fastening. Jewellery accessories are called 'findings' and may be purchased from specialist shops or craft and hobby stores.

~

MATERIALS AND EQUIPMENT

• *small, simple household objects to use as moulds* • *white waste paper* • *electric blender* • *sieve* • *pulp vat* • *plastic bowl* • *newspapers* • *kitchen cloths* • *teaspoon* • *sponge* • *PVA (white) glue* • *glue bowl* • *plastic bag (optional)* • *assorted paintbrushes* • *gouache and acrylic paints* • *pastels* • *inks* • *wax crayons* • *palette* • *non-toxic gold paint* • *copper wire* • *skewer* • *small piece of fabric (optional)* • *metal brooch fastening* • *strong glue*

. . . . . .

1 Make a collection of household objects with interesting shapes from which to cast the brooches. Simple items make the best moulds – for example, buttons, shells and small plastic boxes.

2 Tear the waste paper into postage-stamp-sized pieces. Blend to a pulp with plenty of water, using small handfuls at a time so as not to over-heat the blender's motor. Strain the pulp through a sieve into the vat. Then transfer the pulp into a plastic bowl ready for use.

3 Place your chosen moulds – you will need at least two different sizes and shapes – on a bed of newspaper covered with a damp kitchen cloth. Spoon pulp into the moulds.

4 Use a sponge to press the pulp down into the moulds. The depth of the pulp should be at least 5 mm ($\frac{1}{4}$ in). Leave the moulds to dry in a warm place – this may take a day or two.

5 When the pulp is thoroughly dry, remove the paper shapes from the moulds.

6 Seal the paper shapes with diluted PVA (white) glue (one part glue to one part water), applied with a paintbrush. Work on a plastic bag, if you wish to avoid getting glue on the cloth. Then stick a smaller shape (here a circular one) on to a larger shape.

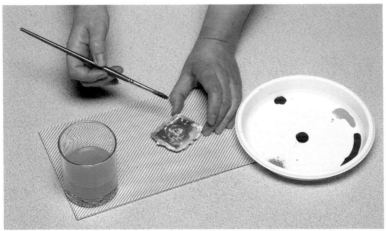

7 Decorate the brooch with gouache and acrylic paints, pastels, inks and wax crayons, depending on which you prefer to use. Build up the layers of colour, taking care not to let them create a muddy effect. Rinse your paintbrush thoroughly when changing to a new colour, and let the paint dry before you add the next colour, as necessary.

8 Add detail to the brooch with gold paint, applied very carefully and quite sparingly with the tip of a paintbrush.

9 Embellish the brooch with short lengths of copper wire formed into swirls by coiling them round a skewer. Stick the swirls in place with undiluted PVA (white) glue. To make the brooch shown here, add a piece of fabric to fill the central area of the circular shape. You could also embellish the brooch with small lengths of silk thread to add coloured highlights and extra texture.

10 Seal the brooch with a coat of diluted PVA (white) glue. When it is thoroughly dry, attach the brooch fastening to the back with strong glue. Ensure that this glue is dry before using.

WATERMARKED LANTERN

JACQUELINE OLDFIELD

A PAPER LANTERN makes an excellent frame for displaying watermarks, which give an elegant, understated touch of decoration to the plainest shade. Watermarks first appeared in sheets of Italian paper during the thirteenth century. They were very simple designs, formed by attaching small shapes made from fine wire to the mesh of the paper-making mould. The wire displaced the paper pulp in that area resulting in a 'watermark' which was clearly visible when held to the light.

~

MATERIALS AND EQUIPMENT

• *pencil* • *paper* • *thin wire* • *pliers* • *deckle and mould* • *needle and thread* • *white waste paper* • *electric blender* • *pulp vat* • *wooden spoon* • *kitchen cloths* • *ruler* • *fire-retardant spray* • *shop-bought paper lantern*

. . . . . .

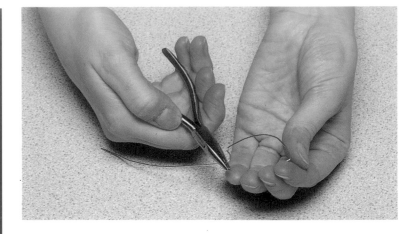

1 First, draw your watermark design on paper, keeping it fairly simple. Following your pattern, bend thin wire to the shape of the design, using a pair of pliers.

2 Stitch the wire watermark firmly in position on top of the mesh of the mould. Hold the wire in place with your fingers, as shown, as you sew from the other side of the mesh.

3 Tear the white waste paper into postage-stamp-sized pieces and blend small handfuls with plenty of water to make a pulp. Pour the pulp into the vat. Add slightly more water than usual – about six parts to one of pulp – stir and then pull a thin sheet of paper. Couch the paper on to a damp kitchen cloth. Pull as many sheets of paper as you need watermarks.

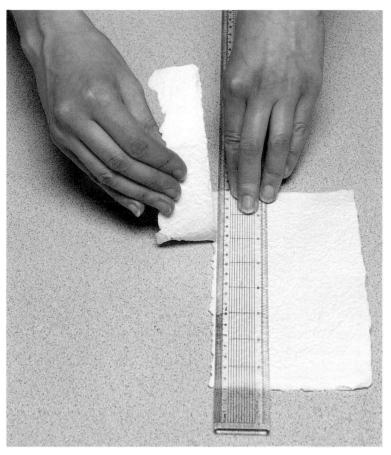

4 Peel each dry sheet of paper from its cloth. Tear the watermarks from the sheets.

5 Coat the paper with fire-retardant spray, following the manufacturer's instructions. Place the strips of paper on the lantern, and carefully stitch each one in position in turn. Never use a lightbulb with a greater wattage than that recommended by the lantern manufacturer.

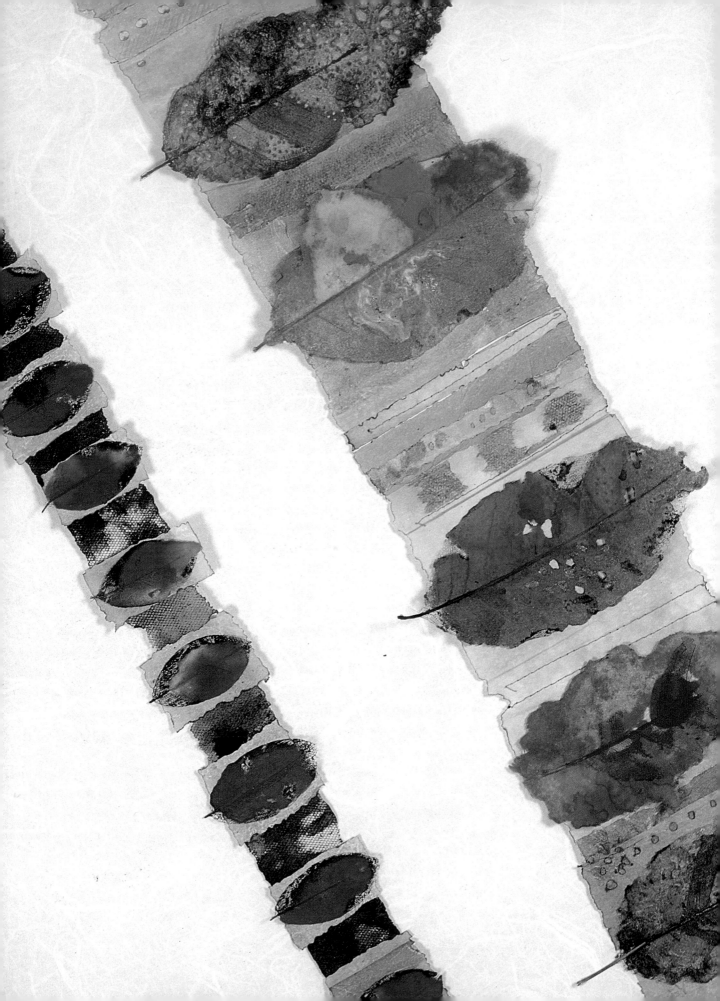

PAPER-LEAF FRIEZE

ELIZABETH COUZINS

THE BRIGHT, jewel-like colours which feature in this unusual wallhanging come from a combination of paints, tissue paper and scraps of rich silk which are applied to a basic paper shape cleverly cast from a leaf skeleton. These delicate skeletons are available from most good florists, and several different shapes may be cast to make a varied design. Once the paper leaves are stuck to their backing sheet, you can add decorative stitching for extra interest and a more textured effect.

~

MATERIALS AND EQUIPMENT

• *white waste paper*
• *electric blender* • *plastic jug* • *leaf skeletons (available from florists)*
• *kitchen cloths*
• *teaspoon* • *sponge*
• *variety of metal or plastic household objects such as the head of a small hammer, nuts, bolts and a paint scraper* • *assorted paintbrushes* • *PVA (white) glue* • *water-based paints* • *scraps of decorated leaves*
• *scraps of silk* • *needle and thread* • *length of tissue paper*
......

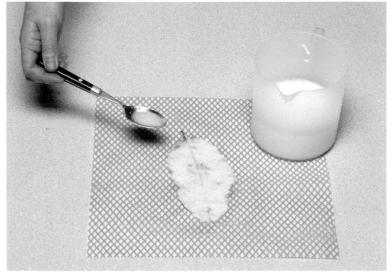

1 Tear the white waste paper into postage-stamp-sized pieces. Blend them to a pulp with plenty of water, resting the blender frequently to avoid over-heating the motor. Transfer the pulp to a plastic jug and pour off most of the water.

2 Put a leaf skeleton on a damp kitchen cloth. Spoon small amounts of pulp on to the leaf to a thickness of about 3 mm ($\frac{1}{8}$ in). Let the pulp soak into the leaf, and sponge off any excess water.

3 While the pulp is still wet,
make patterns by pressing
different household objects,
such as the head of a small
hammer, into it. Leave to dry
in a warm place.

4 When the pulp has dried, seal
the shape by painting the
edges with PVA (white) glue
diluted half-and-half with water.
Leave the glue to dry thoroughly.

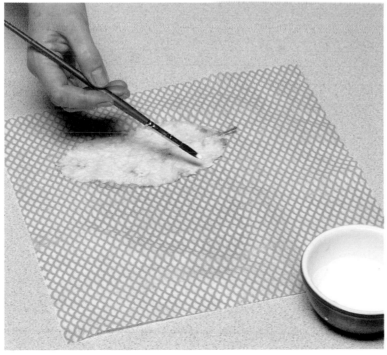

5 Dab colour on to the surface of the dry paper leaf using water-based paints and a sponge. Use several different paints to build up layers of colour, but always rinse the sponge thoroughly before starting with a new colour.

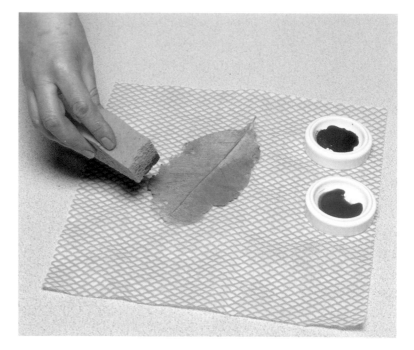

6 To add further decoration, glue on other scraps of decorated leaves.

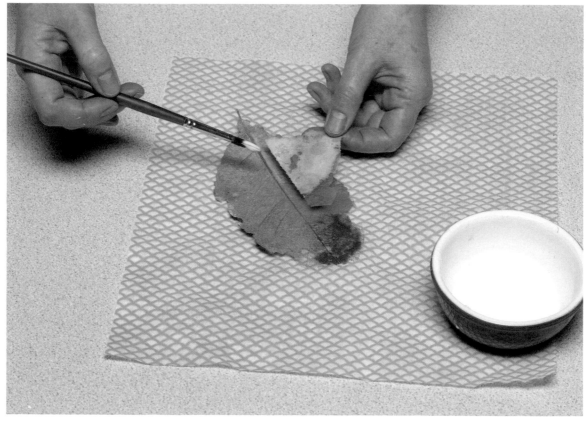

7 To achieve a richly coloured, textured surface, sew scraps of silk to the leaf. Continue to highlight certain areas with decorative stitching worked in contrasting threads.

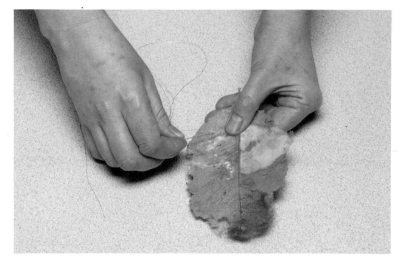

8 To make the backing for the leaf, paint a length of tissue paper with a thin wash of colour. When the paper is dry, you could give it more depth and relief by adding stitching.

9 Stick the leaf to the dry backing with PVA (white) glue. To make a long decorative frieze or wallhanging, simply glue as many paper leaves as you need to the required length of decorated backing tissue, or join individual finished leaves on separate sheets. The sections of tissue may be joined with hand or machine stitching.

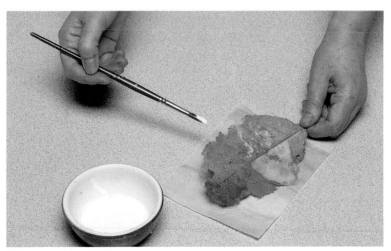

PULP BOWL

GERRY COPP

THESE STUNNING BOWLS are made by an ingenious and simple process. Various bright colours of waste paper are pulped separately, and then formed by hand into bold patterns over a mould. No other type of colouring is used, and the finished appearance of the bowl depends entirely on what paper you use. This technique lends itself very well to a wide range of designs: spots, stripes, stars, hearts and other simple motifs look equally impressive in richly coloured, contrasting pulps.

~

MATERIALS AND EQUIPMENT

• *waste paper in a variety of colours* • *electric blender* • *sieve* • *plastic bowl* • *plastic container* • *wallpaper paste (granules)* • *disposable plastic gloves* • *clear film (plastic wrap)* • *bowl to use as a mould*

. . . . . .

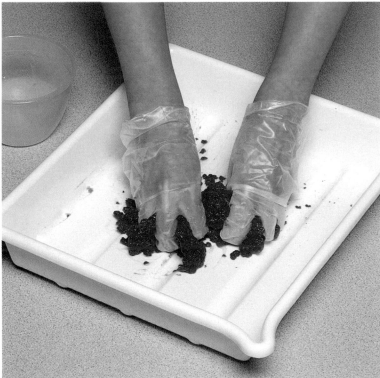

1 Tear one colour of waste paper into postage-stamp-sized pieces, and blend small handfuls with plenty of water to make a pulp. Let the blender rest frequently to avoid over-heating its motor. Strain the pulp through a sieve into the plastic container.

2 In a plastic bowl, mix a small quantity of wallpaper paste (granules) with water to a fairly stiff consistency. Wearing disposable plastic gloves, combine the paste with the strained pulp in the plastic container adding a little paste at a time and mixing until the pulp is a sticky, but not too liquid, mass. Repeat all of the above process for each batch of coloured paper.

3 Cover the back of the bowl chosen as your mould with clear film (plastic wrap). This will ensure easy removal of the pulp bowl once it has dried.

4 Wearing disposable plastic gloves, take a handful of gluey pulp and begin to apply it to the upturned bowl.

5 Continue to apply the pulp to the bowl, gradually building up a pattern. As you add each new colour, push the pulps together gently with your fingertips to ensure that there are no gaps.

6 Leave the bowl to dry in a warm place, then remove it from the back of the mould. Make sure that the inside of the bowl is thoroughly dry before you use it.

TEXTURED-PAPER WALLHANGING

ELIZABETH COUZINS

A VARIETY OF household objects can be used to make simple moulds, which are then cast with thick paper pulp. The resulting shapes make attractive decorative pieces for a wall-hanging, which may be further embellished with additional paper moulded with simple implements to make a lacy, textured surface. This may be emphasized by applying gold paint sparingly to create a more opulent effect.

~

MATERIALS AND EQUIPMENT

* *soaked white waste paper* • *electric blender* • *pulp vat* • *wooden spoon* • *deckle and mould* • *kitchen cloths* • *variety of textured household objects (metal, wood or plastic) such as the head of a hammer or a paint stripper* • *plastic measuring jug* • *old picture frame* • *embroidery hoop (to fit inside picture frame)* • *scissors* • *thin backing paper* • *PVA (white) glue* • *assorted paintbrushes* • *water-based paints* • *sponge* • *paint diffuser (optional)* • *non-toxic gold paint* • *bright silk or tissue paper*

......

1 Blend small handfuls of white waste paper, which has been soaked overnight, to a pulp with plenty of water. Allow the blender to rest frequently to avoid overheating the motor. Pour the pulp into the vat. Pull a fairly thick sheet of paper.

2 Couch the first sheet of paper on to a pile of damp kitchen cloths. Use a household object to make patterns. Leave the sheet to dry naturally on the cloths.

3 Pull a second sheet of thick paper and couch on to more damp kitchen cloths. Make different patterns on this piece. Again, leave the paper to dry naturally on the cloths.

4 Blend another quantity of thick pulp and transfer it to a plastic measuring jug. Make a simple mould by placing the embroidery hoop inside the picture frame on a pile of damp kitchen cloths. Pour the pulp into this mould to produce shaped sheets of paper. Leave the paper to dry thoroughly, then remove the moulds.

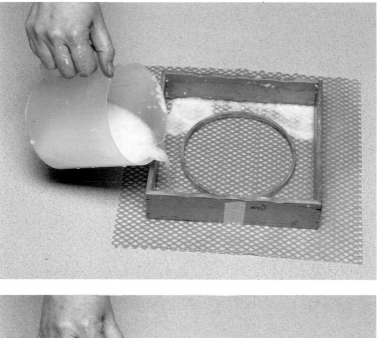

5 Continue to make shaped paper for the central area of the hanging. Give it a textured decorative surface by using household objects, as before. Leave the paper in a warm place to dry thoroughly.

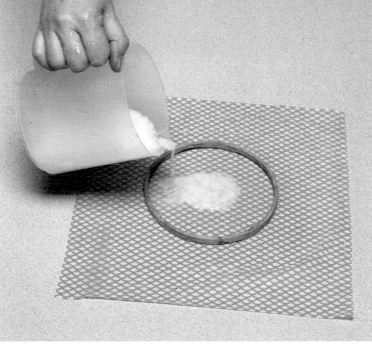

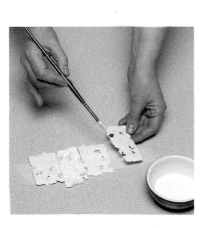

6 Cut the first sheet of decorated paper into strips, and stick them together or attach them to thin backing paper to make the sides of the hanging.

7 Stick the sides of the hanging to the central square of paper, applying the glue carefully with a small paintbrush.

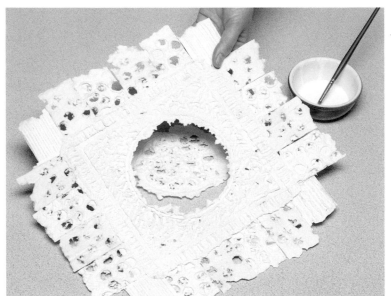

8 Stick this frame over the central circular panel of paper. Seal the whole piece with PVA (white) glue diluted with an equal amount of water. If you wish to further reinforce the hanging, attach backing paper to the underside.

9 Using water-based paints and a sponge, apply colour to the hanging. Alternatively, spray on the paint using a diffuser. Build up layers of paint experimenting with various colours to achieve a subtly glowing depth of tone over the entire hanging.

10 Apply gold highlights to the hanging by rubbing paint over some areas with your fingertips.

11 Add areas of greater detail with a paintbrush to finish and define the different areas of the hanging. Cut a square of bright silk or tissue paper and apply to the back of the central circle so that it is visible through the broken surface.

MARBLED PAPER

JACQUELINE OLDFIELD

MARBLING IS AN ANCIENT craft traditionally used to create decorative endpapers and jackets for books. It is a very simple technique which allows a coloured pattern suspended on water or paste to be transferred to a sheet of paper. The pattern is formed by moving a film of oil paint over the surface of the water until it resembles marble. The pattern may only be transferred once, and can never be repeated exactly, so each sheet of paper is unique.

~

MATERIALS AND EQUIPMENT

- *white waste paper*
- *pulp vat • wooden spoon • deckle and mould*
- *kitchen cloths • pressing boards • g-clamps*
- *shallow tray (large enough to accommodate a sheet of hand-made paper)*
- *wallpaper paste (granules) • oil paints in a variety of colours • glass jars • white spirit (paint thinner) or turpentine*
- *disposable plastic gloves*
- *assorted paintbrushes*
- *cocktail sticks (toothpicks) • newspaper strips • PVA (white) glue*
- *notebook suitable for covering • pencil • ruler*
- *scissors or craft knife*

. . . . . .

1 Blend small handfuls of white waste paper with plenty of water to make a pulp. Pour the pulp into the vat. Pull a sheet of paper. Couch the sheet of paper on to a small pile of damp kitchen cloths. Cover the paper with another damp cloth and place between two pressing boards sealed with g-clamps for about 30 minutes. Remove the pressed paper and leave it on its cloth to dry thoroughly.

2 Fill the shallow tray with water, and mix in enough wallpaper paste (granules) to make quite a thick paste, roughly the consistency of double (heavy) cream.

3 Thin a little of each colour of oil paint in a glass jar with white spirit (paint thinner) or turpentine. The consistency should be even and quite thin. When the colour lands on the surface of the paint it should disperse over the area.

4 Wearing disposable plastic gloves, drop the diluted oil paint, one colour at a time, from a paintbrush on to the surface of the paste in the tray. The colour should drop quite easily from the paintbrush. Alternatively, use a medicine dropper to drop the colour on in a more controlled way.

5 When the surface is evenly covered, spread the paint over the surface of the paste using cocktail sticks (toothpicks). Work quite quickly so that the colours do not mix.

6 Peel the dry sheet of paper carefully from the kitchen cloth. Lower the paper on to the surface of the paste.

7 After a few seconds, remove the paper. The oil paint will have adhered to it, transferring the marbled pattern.

8 Quickly rinse the excess paste from the marbled paper with cold water and leave the sheet to dry on a flat surface. Remove traces of oil paint from the paste in the tray with strips of newspaper, so that you can use it again.

9 When the oil paint is thoroughly dry (this may take up to two or three days), seal the paper with a half-and-half mixture of PVA (white) glue and water, applied with a paintbrush. Leave the paper to dry completely. Place the book to be covered on the wrong side of the paper. Then draw a margin of about 1 cm ($\frac{1}{2}$ in) around the book with a pencil and ruler. Cut the paper to this size.

10 Cut off the corners of the paper, so that when it is stuck on to the cover there will be neat mitred joins and no overlap. Fold the paper back all round the edges of the book cover and stick to the inside with PVA (white) glue. Use the wrong end of a paintbrush to tuck the little flaps of marbled paper into the spine of the book.

SUPPLIERS

CARRIAGE HOUSE PAPER, 79 Guernsey Street, Brooklyn, NY 11222. Telephone for catalogue and orders: (800) 669-8781; telephone for technical assistance: (617) 232-1636. Small and large kits with moulds and deckles; all paper making supplies and equipment.

MAGNOLIA EDITIONS, 2527 Magnolia Street, Oakland, CA 94607. Telephone: (510) 839-5268; catalogue free upon request. All paper making materials and equipment including beginners' kits, beaten or hydrated pulp. Classes available.

LEE S. MCDONALD, INC., P.O. Box 264, Charleston, MA 02129. Telephone: (617) 242-2505; free mail-order catalogue. Suppliers of paper making equipment and kits (including beginners' kits), beaters, presses, drier system, chemicals, pigments, moulds and deckles, cotton linters and sheet pulp and also in ready-to-use form, either dry or wet.

TWINROCKER, P.O. Box 413, Brookston, IN 47923. Telephone: (800) 757-TWIN; telephone for technical assistance: (317) 563-3119. Suppliers of basic moulds and deckles, dry fibres, ready-to-use pulp and kits.

ACKNOWLEDGEMENTS

The author and publishers would like to thank the following people for allowing us to reproduce their photographs: the Ancient Art & Architecture Collection for the pictures on pages 8 and 9, James Copp for the 'Turtle' on page 22 and Vince Bevan for the picture of Gill Clement's jewellery on page 25. The author would like to thank Joanna Lorenz, John Freeman for his photography.

INDEX

A

Additions to pulp, 16

B

Basic techniques, 14–17
Bird box
  materials and equipment, 58
  process, 58–61
Blender, 10
Blending pulp, 16
Bowl, pulp, 79
Brooches, cast, 63–67
Bucket, 11

C

Card, stencilled, 51–55
Cast brooches
  decoration, 63
  materials and equipment, 64
  moulds, 63
  process, 64–67
Couching felts, 11
Couching paper, 15
  materials and equipment, 38
  preparation, 38
  process, 38–41

D

Daffodil paper
  materials and equipment, 38
  process, 38–41
Deckle and mould, 10, 11
Development of paper-
  making, 7

Drying paper, 17
Drying surface, 12

E

Embossed writing paper
  materials and equipment, 48
  process, 48–49
Embossing, 47

F

Findings, 63

G

Gallery, 19–25
Glue, 12
Goggles, 12

H

Hand-made paper, 9
Hollander Beater, 9

L

Laminated leaf paper
  materials and equipment, 44
  process, 44–45
Lamination, 43
Leaf skeletons, 73

M

Marbled paper
  materials and equipment, 90
  process, 90–93
Marbling, 89

Materials and equipment,
  10–13
Mould covering, 11

N

Newspaper, 12

O

Onion skin paper
  materials and equipment, 34
  preparation, 33–34
  process, 34–35

P

Paper leaf frieze
  materials and equipment, 74
  process, 74–77
Paper mills, 8, 9
Papyrus, 7
Parchment, 7
Photographic tray, 12
Plant fibres, 37
  preparing, 17
Post of paper, pressing, 16, 17
Pressing boards, 11
Pulling sheets, 14
Pulp bowl
  materials and equipment, 80
  process, 80–81
PVA glue, 12

R

Recycled paper
  materials and equipment, 28

process, 28–31
Recycling paper, 16
Rubber gloves, 12

S

Sieve, 12
Sizing paper, 17
Stencilled card
  materials and equipment, 52
  process, 52–55
Stencils, making, 51

T

Textured paper wallhanging
  materials and equipment, 84
  moulds, 83
  process, 84–87
Ts'ai Lun, 7

V

Vat, 11
Vellum, 7

W

Wallhanging, textured paper,
  83–87
Wastepaper, 10
Watermarked lantern
  materials and equipment, 70
  process, 70–71
Watermarks, 69
White glue, 12
Writing paper, embossed,
  47–49